NIA

CAROLINA

☆ RALEIGH

FAYETTEVILLE

ALBEMARLE SOUND

PAMLICO SOUND

ATLANTIC OCEAN

N

W ✦ E

S

NORTH CAROLINA,
THE FIRST GOLDEN STATE

TRICIA MARTINEAU WAGNER
ILLUSTRATED BY CANDACE CAMLING

PELICAN PUBLISHING COMPANY

GRETNA 2017

The word "Pelican" and the depiction of a pelican are trademarks of Pelican Publishing Company, Inc., and are registered in the U.S. Patent and Trademark Office.

7105454

Library of Congress Cataloging-in-Publication Data

Names: Wagner, Tricia Martineau, author. | Camling, Candace, illustrator. Title: North Carolina, the first golden state / by Tricia Martineau Wagner ;   illustrations by Candace Camling.
Description: Gretna, Louisiana : Pelican Publishing Company, Inc., [2017]
Identifiers: LCCN 2017004167| ISBN 9781455622733 (hardcover : alk. paper) | ISBN 9781455622740 (e-book)
Subjects: LCSH: North Carolina--Gold discoveries—Juvenile literature. | Gold
  mines and mining—North Carolina—Juvenile literature. | North
  Carolina—History—1775-1865—Juvenile literature.
Classification: LCC F254.3 .W25 2017 | DDC 975.6/03—dc23 LC record available at https://lccn.loc.gov/2017004167

Back-jacket photograph courtesy of Reed Gold Mine, North Carolina Department of Natural and Cultural Resources

Printed in Korea
Published by Pelican Publishing Company, Inc.
1000 Burmaster Street, Gretna, Louisiana 70053

To Kelsey Merreck and Mitchell
Dale Wagner: love you—T. M. W.

To all the pediatric oncology staff
at Blank Children's Hospital. You've
all got hearts of solid gold.—C. C.

Conrad Reed thought he was just about the luckiest boy in Cabarrus County, North Carolina. But he was about to get even luckier.

Like most twelve-year-old boys, Conrad loved to fish. His family's farm had hills to roam and creeks to explore. So when Conrad awoke one beautiful spring day, what did he want to do? Go fishing—if his parents would let him skip church that morning.

As luck would have it, Conrad Reed got his way. He hurried off with two of his sisters to Little Meadow Creek. Little did young Conrad Reed know he would play a big part in America's history on that Sunday morning in 1799. He was about to put Cabarrus County on the map.

The Reed family lived in the backwoods of North Carolina. Their community was made up of German immigrant farmers. Conrad was the third oldest of nine children. Like his father, he was a simple boy from a simple farming family.

When Conrad and his sisters reached the sparkling waters of Little Meadow Creek, he took up his bow and arrow. He began spearing fish hiding along the creek's shady bank.

Suddenly Conrad noticed something odd—a bright yellow rock in the water. It glistened in the sun. Conrad stepped into the creek with his bare feet. A small, shiny, wedge-shaped rock was just beneath the water's surface. Conrad decided to unearth the heavy rock. He carried it home to show his father.

John Reed didn't know what to make of Conrad's seventeen-pound rock. It was far too pretty to throw away. The Reeds began using it as a doorstop. Day after day, month after month, Conrad Reed and his family passed by the rock. It held the door open for three years. No one paid much attention to it.

One day, John Reed became curious. He took the hefty rock with him on a fifteen-mile trip to Concord, North Carolina. He knew a silversmith in town named William Atkinson. The silversmith examined the rock. He didn't know what the shiny metal was either. The rock went back to being the Reeds' doorstop.

In 1802, John Reed looked at the rock again. He took Conrad's rock with him on his yearly 115-mile market trip to Fayetteville. Reed found a jeweler in town. The jeweler instantly knew what the shiny metal was. It was gold. Gold! Gold! Gold!

GOLD! GOLD! GOLD!

The jeweler asked John Reed to leave the nugget with him. He would have it "fluxed," or melted down to separate the gold from the rock. That suited John Reed just fine.

John Reed came back to see the jeweler. The gold had been melted into an "ingot," or solid bar, about seven inches long. The jeweler offered to buy the gold.

John Reed suggested what he thought was a fair price: $3.50—equal to one week of his wages. The jeweler gladly agreed. Conrad's rock was worth more than a thousand times that—$3,600!

News spread about Conrad Reed's gold discovery. Gold! Gold! Gold in Little Meadow Creek! Neighboring farmers found gold on their land too. Soon John Reed learned that the jeweler had cheated him. He went back to Fayetteville. The jeweler gave him an additional $1,200.

John Reed kept farming. And people continued to find gold on his land. In 1803, John Reed started a mining company with three other men. One of his partner's slaves, named Peter, made a huge find: a twenty-eight-pound gold nugget! It was just six inches under the surface of Little Meadow Creek. The nugget was worth $6,600.

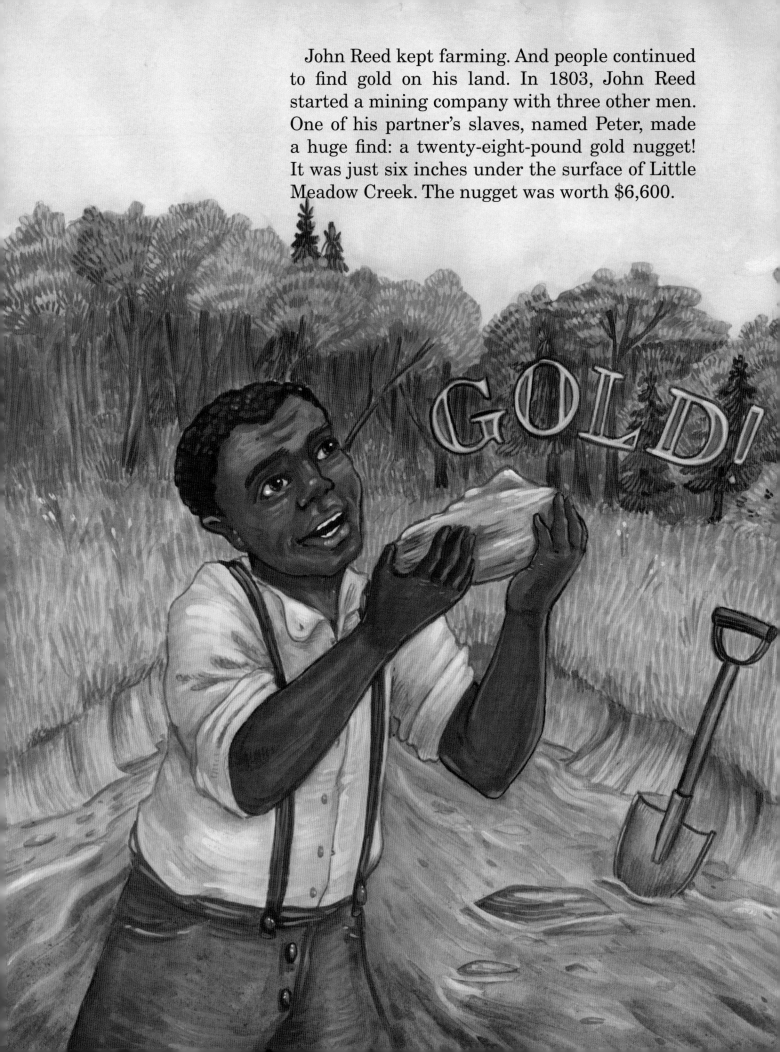

By the 1820s, North Carolina's Gold Rush was on. Gold! Gold! Gold in Cabarrus County! The Reed Mine had produced over two hundred thousand dollars in gold. But Conrad Reed's father was a simple farmer. He had two mining rules: no gold searching until all the crops were in and no clearing of valuable farmland for mining.

Local farmers continued aboveground "placer" or creek mining. They panned for gold in their own creeks, finding nuggets at or near the surface of the water or along the banks. Mining remained a family-run business.

The farmers used shovels and pans. Half-barrel "rockers" were used to sift the heavy gold from the lighter sand in the watery gravel mix.

Gold was discovered in "veins," or layers, of white quartz rocks. In 1825, the Barringer Gold Mine in Montgomery County began underground "lode" mining. They dug deep "shafts" into the earth, with tunnels called "drifts" that branched out.

GOLD! GOLD! GOLD

Soon, news of Conrad's gold discovery traveled overseas. Gold! Gold! Gold in North Carolina! Experienced miners came from England, Europe, and South America. They brought tools and fancy mining equipment. Large Cornish buckets called "kibbles" lifted gold ore and miners up the shafts. Miners worked by candlelight, breaking the rock with picks and shovels. They used gunpowder to blast out rooms to work in, called "stopes."

drift

In 1831, the Reed Mine began underground vein mining. Reaching lode or vein gold was expensive. But John Reed didn't use the latest mining methods or equipment, such as steam pumps or fancy "stamp mills" to pound the rock. Instead, he used horse-driven winding machines called "whims." The whims lifted gold-filled rock up the shafts. Large aboveground stone mills, called "arrastras," crushed the rock to free it of its gold.

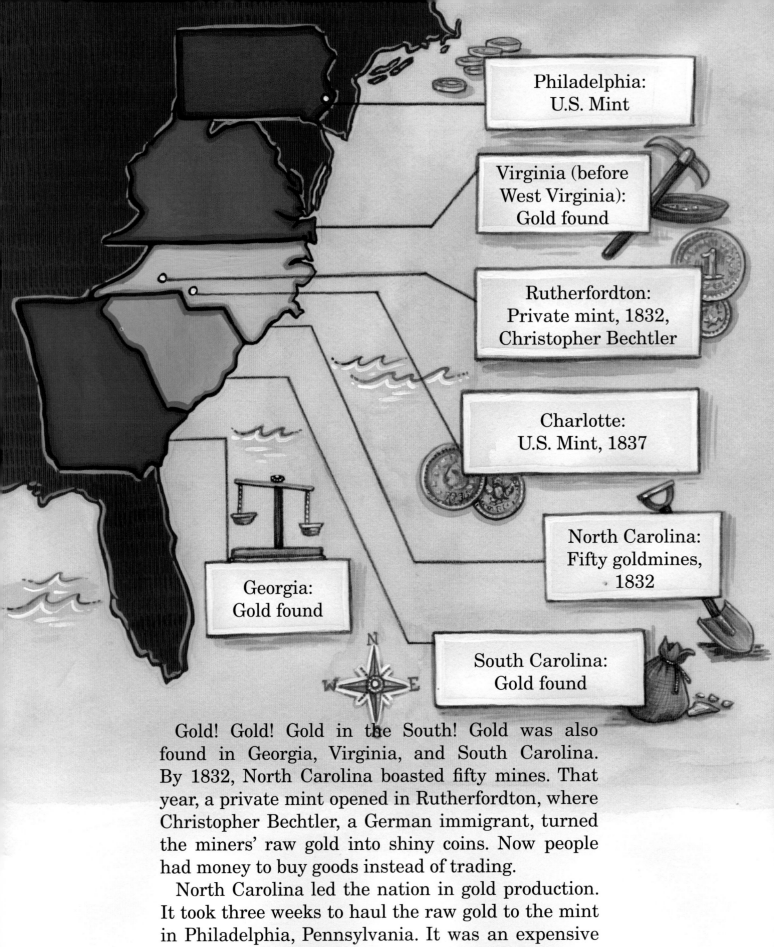

Philadelphia:
U.S. Mint

Virginia (before
West Virginia):
Gold found

Rutherfordton:
Private mint, 1832,
Christopher Bechtler

Charlotte:
U.S. Mint, 1837

North Carolina:
Fifty goldmines,
1832

Georgia:
Gold found

South Carolina:
Gold found

Gold! Gold! Gold in the South! Gold was also found in Georgia, Virginia, and South Carolina. By 1832, North Carolina boasted fifty mines. That year, a private mint opened in Rutherfordton, where Christopher Bechtler, a German immigrant, turned the miners' raw gold into shiny coins. Now people had money to buy goods instead of trading.

North Carolina led the nation in gold production. It took three weeks to haul the raw gold to the mint in Philadelphia, Pennsylvania. It was an expensive and dangerous trip. So in 1837, the United States government opened a mint in Charlotte, North Carolina to make gold coins.

BECHTLER MINT

COIN PRESS

US MINT CHARLOTTE

Conrad Reed grew up and, like his father, remained a simple farmer. Conrad Reed's gold discovery while fishing in Little Meadow Creek in 1799 started America's first Gold Rush—fifty years before California's Gold Rush of 1849!

Glossary

arrastra: A circular mill with a large drag stone used to crush rocks

ARRASTRA

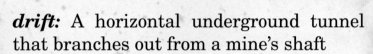
SHAFT
DRIFT

drift: A horizontal underground tunnel that branches out from a mine's shaft

FLUX

flux: A method of separating gold from the rock

INGOT

ingot: Gold that has been molded into a bar that's easy to store or transport

kibble: A big iron bucket used to lift ore and miners to the surface of the mine

KIBBLE

LODE

lode: A large amount of gold in one underground area of rock

MINT

mint: A building where money is coined

ORE

ore: A natural substance or rock found in the earth that contains gold or other minerals

PAN

pan: A shallow metal plate used to wash away dirt and stones from the gold

placer mining: Aboveground mining for gold, at or near the surface of a creek or along its bank, using a pan

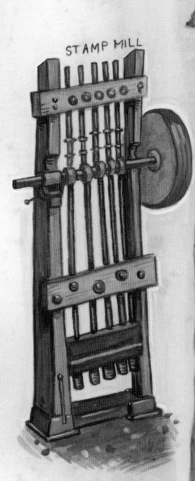

STAMP MILL

ROCKER

rocker: A hollowed log or half-barrel that holds water and gravel and is shaken back and forth to separate gold from the dirt

shaft: A vertical entrance tunnel to a mine, cut deep into the earth

stamp mill: A machine with falling parts made of iron, stone, or wood used to crush rock

stope: An area blasted out of the rock inside the widening tunnel of a mine

vein: A layer of gold within a rock (veins run through rocks like blood vessels)

whim: A horse-driven machine that winds rope around a cylinder to lift rock up a shaft

GOLD VEIN

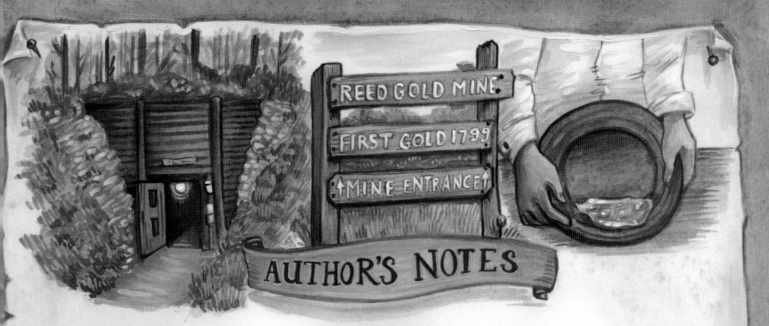

The Reed Gold Mine boasts the first documented gold discovery in the United States. It is now a National Historic Landmark (1966) and a State Historic Site (1971). This Cabarrus County mine is twenty miles east of Charlotte and fifteen miles southeast of Concord. The Reed Gold Mine and visitor center are open to the public. Visitors can tour 400 feet of underground tunnels, pan for gold next to Little Meadow Creek, watch a restored ore-crushing stamp mill in operation, and walk on historic trails. The visitor center has a twenty-minute introductory film about goldmining in North Carolina, along with period mining equipment, historic photographs, gold pieces, and extensive exhibits about mining history and technology.

John Reed had come to America from Germany to help England defeat the colonists during the Revolutionary War. The colonists offered him a seventy-acre land grant to quit the British army. He settled in the backwoods of North Carolina and joined a German immigrant farming community. He married Sarah Kiser and had nine children. Despite the Reed family's wealth from mining, they continued to farm. John Reed rejected outside influences on his mining operation. He refused to spend profits on steam-powered machines or foreign skilled miners. A family argument over who had rights to a thirteen-pound nugget resulted in the Reed Mine being closed from 1834 to 1844. There was no mining until the North Carolina Supreme Court settled the case.

Twelve-year-old Conrad Reed, who discovered the gold in 1799, became a farmer and married the neighboring minister's daughter, Martha Love. They had eight children.

The Reed Gold Mine was sold at public auction after John Reed died, and it changed ownership many times. In 1895, the Kelly family from Ohio bought the Reed Mine.

Nuggets of notable size and purity were unearthed on the Reed property over the years. The last large nugget was found in 1896, just three and a half feet beneath the ground. It weighed twenty-three pounds and was worth $4,800. The family stopped underground mining in 1912.

During the Kelly family's almost eight-decade ownership, they used the abandoned mine's land as a country retreat. Rather than developing or selling the Reed property (about 890 acres), the Kelly heirs preserved it for future generations to enjoy. In 1971, they donated prime land, including the Reed Mine, and the state bought the remaining acres.

The Reed Gold Mine, over two centuries old, is the only major North Carolina mine to stay virtually intact over the years. Gold Hill Mine in Rowan County is now a historic park, the Phoenix Mine in Concord is now Green Oaks Golf Course, and Charlotte's Rudisill Mine lies beneath the city streets. Charlotte's former U.S. Mint building was moved and is now part of the city's Mint Museum of Art.

About one million dollars' worth of gold a year was taken from North Carolina soil during the peak of its Gold Rush. But the mining industry still came in second to farming. North Carolina mining operations gradually spread outside of Cabarrus County to twenty-eight other counties, including Montgomery, Burke, Davidson, Stanly, Rutherford, Rowan, Union, and Mecklenburg (which contained the most mines in the state). The city of Charlotte had many of the most important underground mines, with rich gold veins.

Over six thousand Hessian soldiers from Germany stayed in North Carolina after the Revolutionary War, adding to its cultural development. The discovery of gold in the state brought more immigrants from other countries. This Gold Rush boosted North Carolina's economy and set the stage especially for Charlotte's banking and trade industries.

Before 1849, North Carolina led the nation in gold production, followed by Georgia, Virginia, and South Carolina. However, underground vein mining in North Carolina was expensive and in time tapered off. It was soon eclipsed by the discovery of gold in California in 1848—setting off the nation's second Gold Rush in 1849.

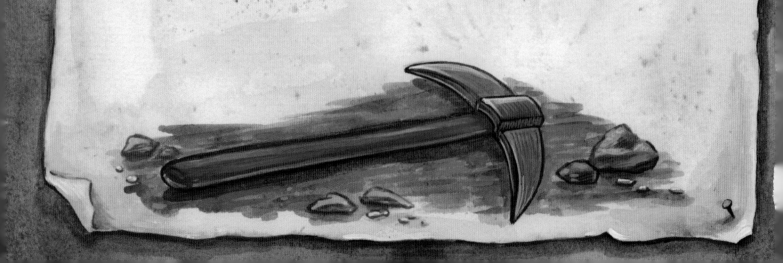

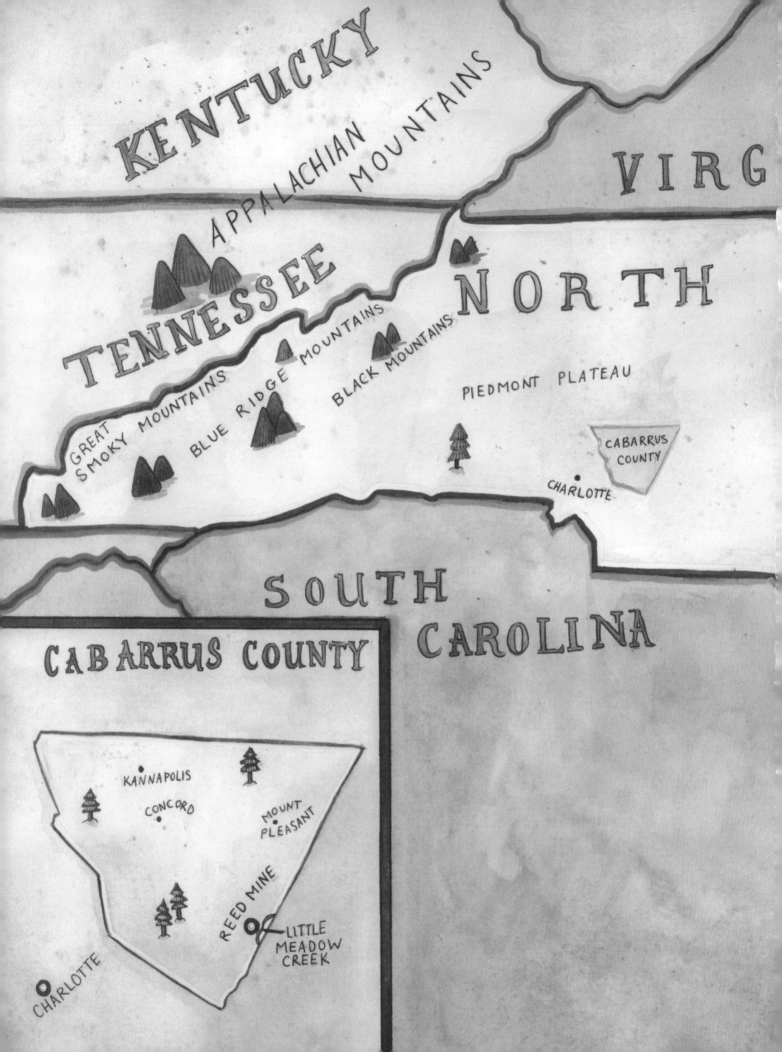